His Holiness the Dalai Lama is a political and religious leader of worldwide renown and winner of the Nobel Peace prize.

D1394625

ALSO BY HIS HOLINESS THE DALAI LAMA

*Freedom in Exile: The Autobiography
of the Dalai Lama*

Ancient Wisdom, Modern World

THE ESSENCE OF
WISDOM

Tenzin Gyatso
His Holiness the Dalai Lama

An *Abacus* Book

First published in Great Britain by Abacus in 2003
The excerpts used in this book are from
Ancient Wisdom, Modern World

A CIP catalogue record for this book is
available from the British Library.

ISBN 0 349 11646 6

Typeset in Dante by M Rules
Printed and bound in Great Britain by
William Clowes Ltd

Abacus
An imprint of
Time Warner Books UK
Brettenham House
Lancaster Place
London WC2E 7EN

www.TimeWarnerBooks.co.uk

*I*n the past, the respect people had for religion meant that ethical practice was maintained through a majority following one religion or another. But this is no longer the case. We must therefore find some other way of establishing basic ethical principles.

*T*o suppose that merely by abandoning material progress we could overcome all our problems would be short-sighted. That would be to ignore their underlying causes. Besides, there is much in the modern world to be optimistic about.

I have come to the conclusion that whether or not a person is a religious believer does not matter much. Far more important is that they be a good human being.

For me, Buddhism remains the most precious path. It corresponds best to my personality. But that does not mean I believe it to be the best religion for everyone any more than I believe it necessary for everyone to be a religious believer.

*T*here is an important distinction to be made between religion and spirituality. Religion I take to be concerned with faith in the claims to salvation of one faith tradition or another, an aspect of which is acceptance of some form of metaphysical or supernatural reality, including perhaps an idea of heaven or *nirvana*. Spirituality I take to be concerned with those qualities of the human spirit – such as love and compassion, patience, tolerance, forgiveness, contentment, a sense of responsibility, a sense of harmony – which brings happiness to both self and others. This is why I sometimes say that religion is something we can perhaps do without. What we cannot do without are these basic spiritual qualities.

[4]

The one who is compassionate, loving, patient, tolerant, forgiving and so on to some extent recognizes the potential impact of their actions on others and orders their conduct accordingly. Thus spiritual practice involves, on the one hand, acting out of concern for others' well-being. On the other, it entails transforming ourselves so that we become more readily disposed to do so. To speak of spiritual practice in any terms other than these is meaningless.

What is the relationship between spirituality and ethical practice? Since love and compassion and similar qualities all, by definition, presume some level of concern for others' well-being, they also presume ethical restraint. We cannot be loving and compassionate unless at the same time we curb our own harmful impulses and desires.

*E*stablishing binding ethical principles is possible when we take as our starting point the observation that we all desire happiness and wish to avoid suffering. We have no means of discriminating between right and wrong if we do not take into account others' feelings, others' suffering. For this reason, ethical conduct is not something we engage in because it is somehow right in itself but because, like ourselves, all others desire happiness and to avoid suffering.

When the driving force of our actions is wholesome, our actions will tend automatically to contribute to others' well-being. They will thus automatically be ethical.

We find that the more we succeed in transforming our hearts and minds through cultivating spiritual qualities, the better able we will be to cope with adversity and the greater the likelihood that our actions will be ethically wholesome.

A spiritual revolution entails an ethical revolution.

When we consider reality itself, we quickly become aware of its infinite complexity, and we realize that our habitual perception of it is often inadequate. If this were not so, the concept of deception would be meaningless. If things and events always unfolded as we expected, we would have no notion of illusion or of misconception.

*I*f it is true that no object or phenomena, not even the self, exists inherently, should we then conclude that, ultimately, nothing exists at all? Or is the reality we perceive simply a projection of the mind, apart from which nothing exists? No. When we say that things and events are without intrinsic reality, we are not denying the existence of phenomena altogether. The 'identitylessness' of phenomena points rather to the way in which things exist: not independently but in a sense interdependently.

While acknowledging that there is often a discrepancy between perception and reality, it is important not to go to the extreme of supposing that behind the phenomenal is a realm which is somehow more 'real'. The problem with this is that we may then dismiss everyday experience as nothing but an illusion. That would be quite wrong.

*T*here is no self-interest completely unrelated to others' interests.

Because our interests are inextricably linked, we are compelled to accept ethics as the indispensable interface between my desire to be happy and yours.

*A*n ethical act is one which does not harm others' experience or expectation of happiness.

So far as actual possessions are concerned, for example, we must admit that often they cause us more, not less, difficulties in life. The car breaks down, we lose our money, our most precious belongings are stolen, our house is damaged by fire. Either that or we suffer because we worry about these things happening.

When we act to fulfil our immediate desires without taking into account others' interests, we undermine the possibility of lasting happiness.

*T*he principal characteristic of genuine happiness is peace: inner peace. By this I do not mean some kind of feeling of being 'spaced out'. Nor am I speaking of an absence of feeling. On the contrary, the peace I am describing is rooted in concern for others and involves a high degree of sensitivity and feeling.

*I*f we can develop this quality of inner peace, no matter what difficulties we meet with in life, our basic sense of well-being will not be undermined. Though there is no denying the importance of external factors in bringing this about, we are mistaken if we suppose that they can ever make us completely happy.

*D*eveloping inner peace, on which lasting – and therefore – meaningful happiness is dependent, is like any other task in life: we have to identify its causes and conditions and then diligently set about cultivating them.

There is an important distinction to be made between what we might call ethical and spiritual acts. An ethical act is one where we refrain from causing harm to others' experience or expectation of happiness. Spiritual acts we can describe in terms of those qualities mentioned earlier of love, compassion, patience, forgiveness, humility, tolerance and so on which presume some level of concern for others' well-being.

We humans are social beings. We come into the world as the result of others' actions. We survive here in dependence on others. Whether we like it or not, there is hardly a moment of our lives when we do not benefit from others' activities. So it is hardly surprising that most of our happiness arises in the context of our relationships with others. Nor is it so remarkable that our greatest joy should come when we are motivated by concern for others. But that is not all. We find that not only do altruistic actions bring about happiness, but they also lessen our experience of suffering.

*B*ecause our every action has a universal dimension, a potential impact on others' happiness, ethics are necessary as a means to ensure that we do not harm others.

Genuine happiness consists in those spiritual qualities of love and compassion, patience, tolerance, forgiveness, humility and so on. It is these which provide happiness both for ourselves and for others.

We have a need for others' kindness which runs like a thread throughout our whole life. It is most apparent when we are young and when we are old. But we have only to fall ill to be reminded of how important it is to be loved and cared about even during our prime years. Though it may seem a virtue to be able to do without affection, in reality a life lacking this precious ingredient must be a miserable one.

*F*or me, human beings' ability to smile is one of our most beautiful characteristics. Personally, I always feel a bit curious when I smile at someone and they remain serious and unresponding. On the other hand, my heart is gladdened when they reciprocate. Even in the case of someone I have nothing to do with, when that person smiles at me, I am touched. But why? The answer surely is that a genuine smile touches something fundamental in us: our natural appreciation of kindness.

*P*erhaps one of the reasons for the popularity of the belief that human nature is aggressive lies in our continual exposure to bad news through the media. Yet the very cause of this is surely that good news is not news.

Our innate capacity for empathy is the source of that most precious of all qualities, which in Tibetan we call *nying je* or compassion.

When we act out of concern for others, our behaviour towards them is automatically positive. This is because we have no room for suspicion when our hearts are filled with love. It is as if an inner door is opened, allowing us to reach out.

*T*he world's major religious traditions each give the development of love and compassion a key role. Because they are both the source and the result of patience, tolerance, forgiveness and all good qualities, their importance is considered to extend from the beginning to the end of spiritual practice. But even without a religious perspective, love and compassion are clearly of fundamental importance to us all.

*D*eveloping the compassion on which happiness depends demands a two-pronged approach. On the one hand, we need to restrain those factors which inhibit compassion. On the other, we need to cultivate those which are conducive to it. We find that by transforming our habits and dispositions we can begin to perfect our overall state of heart and mind – that from which all our actions spring. The first thing, then – because the spiritual qualities conducive to compassion entail positive ethical conduct – is to cultivate a habit of inner discipline.

*U*nlike physical discipline, true inner – or spiritual – discipline cannot be achieved by force but only through voluntary and deliberate effort based on understanding. In other words, conducting ourselves ethically consists in more than merely obeying laws and precepts.

*I*f hatefulness were an unchangeable characteristic of consciousness, then consciousness must always be hateful. Clearly this is not the case. There is an important distinction to be made between consciousness as such and the thoughts and emotions it experiences.

We can conceive of the nature of mind in terms of the water in a lake. When the water is stirred up by a storm, the mud from the lake's bottom clouds it, making it appear opaque. But the nature of the water is not dirty. When the storm passes, the mud settles and the water is left clear once again. So although generally we may suppose mind, or consciousness, to be an inherent and unchangeable entity, when we consider it more deeply, we see that it consists in a whole spectrum of events and experiences.

This observation, that emotion and consciousness are not the same thing, tells us that we do not have to be controlled by our thoughts and emotions.

We might think of mind, or consciousness, in terms of a president or monarch who is very honest, very pure. On this view, our thoughts and emotions are like cabinet ministers. Some of them give good advice, some bad. Some have the well-being of others as their principal concern, others only their own narrow interests.

*N*egative thoughts and emotions obstruct our most basic aspiration – to be happy and to avoid suffering. When we act under their influence, we become oblivious to the impact our actions have on others: they are thus the cause of our destructive behaviour both toward others and to ourselves. They are the very source of unethical conduct.

*T*hough there may be a few exceptions, we find that if a person lives a very selfish life, without concern for others' welfare, they tend to become quite lonely and miserable. Though they may be surrounded by people who are friends of their wealth or status, when the selfish or aggressive individual faces tragedy, not only do these so-called friends vanish, they may even secretly rejoice.

We need to pay close attention and be aware of our body and its actions, of our speech and what we say, and of our hearts and minds and what we think and feel. We must be on the lookout for the slightest negativity and keep asking ourselves such questions as, 'Am I happier when my thoughts and emotions are negative and destructive or when they are wholesome?', 'What is the nature of consciousness? Does it exist in and of itself, or does it exist in dependence on other factors?', We need to think, think, think. We should be like a scientist who collects data, analyses it, and draws the appropriate conclusion.

Gaining insight into our own negativity is a lifelong task, and one which is capable of almost infinite refinement. But unless we undertake it, we will be unable to see where to make the necessary changes in our lives.

*T*he afflictive emotions also have an irrational dimension. They encourage us to suppose that appearances are invariably commensurate with reality. When we become angry or feel hatred, we tend to relate to others as if their characteristics were immutable. A person can appear to be objectionable from the crown of their head to the soles of their feet. We forget that they, like us, are merely suffering human beings with the same wish to be happy and to avoid suffering as we ourselves.

Nowhere is the uselessness of afflictive emotion more obvious than in the case of anger. When we become angry, we stop being compassionate, loving, generous, forgiving, tolerant and patient altogether. We thus deprive ourselves of the very things that happiness consists in.

*N*egative thoughts and emotions are what cause us to act unethically.

*T*here is an important distinction to be made between denial and restraint. The latter constitutes a deliberate and voluntarily adopted discipline based on an appreciation of the benefits of doing so.

*I*t is far better to confront a person or situation than to hide our anger away, brood on it and nurture resentment in our hearts. Yet if we indiscriminately express negative thoughts and emotions simply on the grounds that they must be articulated, there is a strong possibility, for all the reasons I have given, that we will lose control and overreact. Thus the important thing is to be discriminating, both in terms of the feelings we express and in how we express them.

Genuine happiness is characterized by inner peace and arises in the context of our relationships with others. It therefore depends on ethical conduct. This in turn consists in acts which take others' well-being into account. If, then, we wish to be happy, we need to curb our response to negative thoughts and emotions. We are not talking about attaining Buddhahood here, we are not talking about God. We are merely recognizing that my interests and future happiness are closely connected to others' and learning to act accordingly.

*I*f we are to be genuinely happy, inner restraint is indispensable. But as well as refraining from negative thoughts and emotions, we need to cultivate and reinforce our positive qualities. What are these positive qualities? The basic human, or spiritual, qualities of love and compassion, patience, tolerance, humility, forgiveness and so on.

*P*atient forbearance, then, is the quality which enables us to prevent negative thoughts and emotions from taking hold of us. It safeguards our peace of mind in the face of adversity. Through practising patience in this way, our conduct is rendered ethically wholesome. The first step in ethical practice is to check our response to negative thoughts and emotions as they arise. The next step – what we do after applying the brakes – is to counter that provocation with patience.

*F*or every negative state, we find that we can identify one which opposes it. For example, humility opposes pride; contentment opposes greed, perseverance opposes indolence. If, therefore, we wish to overcome the unwholesome states which arise when negative thoughts and emotions are allowed to develop, cultivating virtue should not be seen as separate from restraining our response to afflictive emotion. They go hand in hand.

The first step in overcoming anxiety is to develop a proper perspective of our situation. This we can do in a number of different ways. One of the most effective is to try to shift the focus of attention away from self and toward others. When we succeed in this, we find that the scale of our own problems diminishes. This is not to say we should ignore our own needs altogether, but rather that we should try to remember others' needs alongside our own, no matter how pressing ours may be. This is helpful, because when our concern for others is translated into action, we find that confidence arises automatically and worry and anxiety diminish.

*A*lmost all the mental and emotional suffering which is such a feature of modern living – including the sense of hopelessness, of loneliness and so on – lessen the moment we begin to engage in actions motivated by concern for others.

*A*s a general principle, it is essential to avoid extremes. Just as overeating is as dangerous as undereating, so it is with the pursuit and practice of virtue. We find that even noble causes when carried to extremes can become a source of harm.

*T*he cultivation of generosity is essential to counteract our tendency to guard our possessions and even our energy too closely. The practice of giving helps us to overcome our habit of miserliness, which we tend to justify by asking, 'What will I have for myself if I start giving things away?'

Just as there is clearly a distinction between valid confidence, in the sense of self-esteem, and conceit – which we can describe as an inflated sense of importance grounded in a false image of self – so it is important to distinguish between genuine humility, which is a species of modesty, and a lack of confidence. They are not the same thing at all, though many confuse them.

Those who are religiously minded must understand that there is no blessing or initiation – which, if only we could receive it – nor any mysterious or magical formula or mantra or ritual – if only we could discover it – that can enable us to achieve transformation instantly. It comes little by little, just as a building is constructed brick by brick. There are no shortcuts.

While it is good to raise our sights as we progress, it is a mistake to judge our behaviour by using the ideal as a standard, just as it would be foolish to judge our child's performance as a first-year student from the perspective of a graduate. For this reason, far more effective than short bursts of heroic effort followed by periods of laxity is to work steadily like a stream flowing toward our goal of transformation.

Whereas the fundamental questions of human existence, such as why we are here, where we are going and whether the universe had a beginning, have each elicited different responses in different philosophical traditions, it is self-evident that a generous heart and wholesome actions lead to greater peace. And it is equally clear that their negative counterparts bring undesirable consequences.

*H*appiness arises from virtuous causes. If we truly desire to be happy, there is no other way to proceed but by way of virtue: it is the method by which happiness is achieved. And, we might add, the basis of virtue, its ground, is ethical discipline.

*T*here is nothing exceptional about acts of charity toward those we already feel close to.

*I*f our love for someone is based largely on attraction, whether it be their looks or some other superficial characteristic, our feelings for that person are liable, over time, to evaporate. When they lose the quality we found alluring, the situation can change completely, this despite their being the same person. This is why intimate relationships based purely on attraction are almost always unstable.

When we begin to develop a genuine appreciation of the value of compassion, our outlook on others begins automatically to change. This alone can serve as a powerful influence on the conduct of our lives.

Most people, including myself, must struggle to reach the point where putting others' interests on a par with our own becomes easy. We should not allow this to put us off, however. For while undoubtedly there will be obstacles on the way to developing a genuinely warm heart, there is the deep consolation of knowing that in doing so we are creating the conditions for our own happiness.

*H*ow are we to attain happiness? With violence and aggression? Of course not. With money? Perhaps up to a point, but no further. But with love, by sharing in others' suffering, by recognizing ourselves clearly in all others – especially those who are disadvantaged and those whose rights are not respected – by helping others to be happy: yes.

*T*here is nothing amazing about being highly educated, there is nothing amazing about being rich. Only when the individual has a warm heart do these attributes become worthwhile.

*E*thically wholesome actions arise naturally
in the context of compassion.

Nearly every worldly pleasure comes to harm us when carried to an extreme. This is why contentment is indispensable if we are to be genuinely happy.

*T*o suppose that *karma* is some sort of independent energy which predestines the course of our whole life is simply incorrect. Who creates *karma*? We ourselves. In everything we do, there is cause and effect. We cannot, therefore, throw up our hands whenever we find ourselves confronted by unavoidable suffering. To say that every misfortune is simply the result of *karma* is tantamount to saying that we are totally powerless in life. If this were correct, there would be no cause for hope. We might as well pray for the end of the world.

*T*he degree to which suffering affects us is largely up to us. When we look at a particular problem from close up, it tends to fill our whole field of vision and look enormous. If, however, we look at the same problem from a distance, automatically we will start to see it in relation to other things. This simple act makes a tremendous difference. It enables us to see that though a given situation may truly be tragic, even the most unfortunate event has innumerable aspects and can be approached from many different angles. Indeed, it is very rare, if not impossible, to find a situation which is negative no matter how we look at it.

*I*f we can shift our focus away from self and toward others, we experience a freeing effect. There is something about the dynamics of self-absorption, or worrying about ourselves too much, which tends to magnify our suffering. Conversely, when we came to see it in relation to others' suffering, we begin to recognize that, relatively speaking, it is not all that unbearable. This enables us to maintain our peace of mind much more easily than if we concentrate on our problems to the exclusion of all else.

*I*t is worth remembering that the time of greatest gain in terms of wisdom and inner strength is often that of greatest difficulty.

*T*here is a natural tendency for wealth to spoil us. The result is that we find it progressively more difficult to bear easily the problems everyone must encounter from time to time.

*I*f we try to avoid or deny a given problem by simply ignoring it or taking to drink or drugs, or even some forms of meditation or prayer, as a means of escape, while there is a chance of short-term relief, the problem itself remains. Such an approach is simply avoiding the issue, not resolving it.

We are mistaken if we ever suppose that our experience of suffering – or happiness, for that matter – can be attributed to a single source. Everything that arises does so within the context of innumerable causes and conditions. If this was not so, as soon as we came into contact with something that we considered good, automatically we would become happy, whenever we came into contact with something that we considered bad, automatically we would become sad. But that is not reality.

*U*nfortunate events, though potentially a source of anger and despair, have equal potential to be a source of spiritual growth. Whether or not this is the outcome depends on our response.

*E*thical discipline is indispensable because it is the means by which we mediate between the competing claims of my right to happiness and all others' equal right.

*L*ove and compassion, patience, tolerance and forgiveness are essential qualities. When they are present in our lives, everything we do becomes an instrument to benefit the whole human family. Even in terms of our daily occupation – whether this is looking after children in the home, working in a factory, or serving the community as a doctor, lawyer, business person or teacher – our actions contribute towards the well-being of all.

Given the complex nature of reality, it is very difficult to say that a particular act or type of act is right or wrong in itself. Ethical conduct is thus not something we engage in because it is somehow right in itself. We do so because we recognize that, just as I desire to be happy and to avoid suffering, so do all others.

I believe it is very useful to have a set of basic ethical precepts to guide us in our daily lives. These can help us to form good habits, although I should add my opinion that in adopting such precepts, it is perhaps best to think of them less in terms of moral legislation than as reminders always to keep others' interests at heart and in the forefront of our minds. The consensus among both the world's great religions and the greater part of the humanist philosophical tradition, despite differences of opinion concerning metaphysical grounding, is to my mind compelling. All agree on the negativity of killing, stealing, telling lies and sexual misconduct. In addition, all agree on the need to avoid hatred, pride, covetousness, envy, greed, lust, harmful ideologies (such a racism) and so on.

*E*thically wholesome conduct depends on us applying the principle of non-harming. However, there are bound to be situations where any course of action would appear to involve breaking a precept. Under such circumstances, we must use our intelligence to judge which course of action will be least harmful in the long run.

*T*he moral value of a given act is to be judged in relation both to time, place and circumstance and to the interests of the totality of all others in the future as well as now. So while a given act is ethically sound under one set of circumstances, the same act at another time and place and under a different set of circumstances may not be.

*I*t is far more useful to be aware of a single shortcoming in ourselves than it is to be aware of a thousand in somebody else. For when the fault is our own, we are in a position to correct it.

As someone who believes in the continuation of consciousness after the death of the body, I would argue that it is much better to have pain with this human body. At least we can benefit from the care of others, whereas, if we choose to die, we may find that we have to endure suffering in some other form.

*E*xercising our critical faculties in the ethical realm entails taking responsibility both for our acts and for their underlying motives. If we do not take responsibility for our motives, whether positive or negative, the potential for harm is much greater. Each act affects not only the people closest to us but our friends, colleagues, community and ultimately the world.

*I*n the past, families and small communities could exist more or less independently of one another. If they took into account their neighbours' well-being, so much the better. Yet they could survive quite well without this kind of perspective. Such is no longer the case. Today's reality is so complex and, on the material level at least, so clearly interconnected that a different outlook is needed.

To develop a sense of universal responsibility – of the universal dimension of our every act and of the equal right of all others to happiness and not to suffer – is to develop an attitude of mind whereby, if we see an opportunity to benefit others, we will take it in preference to merely looking after our own narrow interests.

When we neglect others' well-being and ignore the universal dimension of our actions, it is inevitable that we will come to see our interests as separate from theirs. We will overlook the fundamental oneness of the human family.

When we put too much emphasis on superficial differences, and on account of them make small rigid discriminations, we cannot avoid bringing about additional suffering both for ourselves and others. This makes no sense. We humans already have enough problems. We all face death, old age and sickness – not to mention the inevitability of meeting with disappointment. Is this not enough?

*I*f we choose not to modify our behaviour out of respect for others' equal right to happiness and not to suffer, it will not be long before we begin to notice the negative consequences. Imagine the pollution of an extra two billion cars, for example. It would affect us all. So contentment is not merely an ethical matter. If we do not wish to add to our own experience of suffering, it is a matter of necessity.

I believe that the culture of perpetual economic growth needs to be questioned. In my view it fosters discontent, and with this comes a great number of problems, both social and environmental.

*U*niversal responsibility also leads us to commitment to the principle of honesty. What do I mean by this? We can think of honesty and dishonesty in terms of the relationship between appearance and reality. Sometimes these synchronize, often they do not. But when they do, that is honesty, as I understand it. So we are honest when our actions are what they seem to be.

When we commit ourselves to honesty, we help reduce the level of misunderstanding, doubt and fear throughout society. In a small but significant way, we create the conditions for a happy world.

We must avoid, at all cost, the urge to shut away those who are grievously afflicted as if they were a burden. The same goes for those who are diseased or marginalized. To push them away would be to heap suffering on suffering. If we ourselves were in the same condition, we would look to others for help. Indeed, the affection we show to such people is, in my opinion, the measure of our spiritual health, both at the level of the individual and at that of society.

*A*lthough it will undoubtedly be difficult to bring about genuine peace and harmony, clearly it can be done. The potential is there. And its foundation is a sense of responsibility on the part of each of us as individuals towards all others.

*R*ecently I was told that the number of billionaires in America had increased from seventeen just a few years ago to several hundred today. Yet at the same time, the poor remain poor and in some cases are becoming poorer. This I consider to be completely immoral. While millions do not even have the basic necessities of life – adequate food, shelter, education and medical facilities – the inequity of wealth distribution is a scandal.

When a person is born rich, or acquires wealth by some other means, they have a tremendous opportunity to benefit others. What a waste when that opportunity is squandered on self-indulgence.

*T*he world will change when each individual makes the attempt to counter their negative thoughts and emotions and when we practice compassion for its inhabitants irrespective of whether or not we have direct relationships with them.

*K*nowledge is important, but much more important is the use towards which it is put. This depends on the heart and mind of the one who uses it.

*I*f we had to choose between learning and virtue, the latter is definitely more valuable. The good heart which is the fruit of virtue is by itself a great benefit to humanity. Mere knowledge is not.

The natural world is our home. It is not necessarily sacred or holy. It is simply where we live. It is therefore in our interests to look after it.

We humans are the only species with the power to destroy the earth as we know it. The birds have no such power, nor do the insects, nor does any mammal. Yet if we have the capacity to destroy the earth, so, too, do we have the capacity to protect it.

*T*he idea of not having children just because we want to enjoy a full life without responsibility is quite mistaken I think.

Chairman Mao once said that political power comes from the barrel of a gun. Of course it is true that violence can achieve certain short-term objectives. But it cannot obtain long-lasting ends. If we look at history, we find that in time, humanity's love of peace, justice and freedom always triumphs over cruelty and oppression. This is why I am such a fervent believer in non-violence.

We each have a role to play in creating a climate for genuine peace. When, as individuals, we disarm ourselves internally – through countering our negative thoughts and emotions and cultivating positive qualities – we create the conditions for external disarmament.

Given human beings' love of truth, justice, peace and freedom, creating a better, more compassionate world is a genuine possibility. The potential is there.

*I*rrespective of doctrinal and other differences, all the major world religions are concerned with helping individuals to become good human beings. All emphasize love and compassion, patience, tolerance, forgiveness, humility and so on, and all are capable of helping individuals to develop these.

*I*t is essential to realize that religious practice entails a lot more than merely saying, 'I believe' or, as in Buddhism, 'I take refuge'. There is also more to it than just visiting temples, or shrines or churches. And taking religious teachings is of little benefit if they do not enter the heart but remain at the level of intellect alone.

*T*he efforts we make sincerely to transform ourselves are what make us a genuine religious practitioner.

*I*t is unhelpful to try to argue on the basis of philosophy or metaphysics that one religion is better than another.

*T*o my way of thinking, the diversity that exists amongst the various religious traditions is enormously enriching. There is thus no need to try to find ways of saying that ultimately all religions are the same. They are similar in that they all emphasize the indispensability of love and compassion in the context of ethical discipline. But to say this is not to say that they are all essentially one.

I do not advocate a 'super' or a new 'world' religion. It would mean that we would lose the unique characteristics of the different faith traditions.

The whole purpose of religion is to facilitate love and compassion, patience, tolerance, humility, forgiveness and so on. If we neglect these, changing our religion will be of no help. In the same way, even if we are fervent believers in our own faith, it will avail us nothing if we neglect to implement these qualities in our daily lives. Such a believer is no better off than a patient with some fatal illness who merely reads a medical treatise but fails to undertake the treatment prescribed.

*T*ime passes unhindered. When we make mistakes, we cannot turn the clock back and try again. All we can do is use the present well.

*I*f when our final day comes we are able to look back and see that we have lived full, productive and meaningful lives, that will at least be of some comfort. If we cannot, we may be very sad. But which of these we experience is up to us.

*T*he best way to ensure that when we approach death we do so without remorse is to ensure that in the present moment we conduct ourselves responsibly and with compassion for others. Actually, this is in our own interest, and not just because it will benefit us in the future.

Compassion is what makes our life meaningful. It is the source of all lasting happiness and joy. And it is the foundation of a good heart, the heart of one who acts out of a desire to help others. Through kindness, through affection, through honesty, through truth and justice towards all others we ensure our own benefit. This is not a matter for complicated theorizing. It is a matter of common sense.

We can reject everything else: religion, ideology, all received wisdom. But we cannot escape the necessity of love and compassion.

*L*ove for others and respect for their rights and dignity, no matter who or what they are: ultimately these are all we need. So long as we practise these in our daily lives, then no matter if we are learned or unlearned, whether we believe in Buddha or God, or follow some other religion or none at all, as long as we have compassion for others and conduct ourselves with restraint out of a sense of responsibility, there is no doubt we will be happy.

*I*n focusing on the mundane, what is essential remains hidden from us. Of course, if we could be truly happy doing so, then it would be entirely reasonable to live like this. Yet we cannot.

If in the midst of your enjoyment of the world you have a moment, try to help in however small a way those who are downtrodden and those who, for whatever reason, cannot or do not help themselves. Try not to turn away from those whose appearance is disturbing, from the ragged and unwell. Try never to think of them as inferior to yourself. If you can, try not even to think of yourself as better than the humblest beggar. You will look the same in your grave.

*T*his short prayer gives me great inspiration in my quest to benefit others:

May I become at all times, both now and forever
A protector for those without protection
A guide for those who have lost their way
A ship for those with oceans to cross
A bridge for those with rivers to cross
A sanctuary for those in danger
A lamp for those without light
A place of refuge for those who lack shelter
And a servant to all in need.